dreamers

THE BOY
WHO MADE
MAGIC

This book belongs to

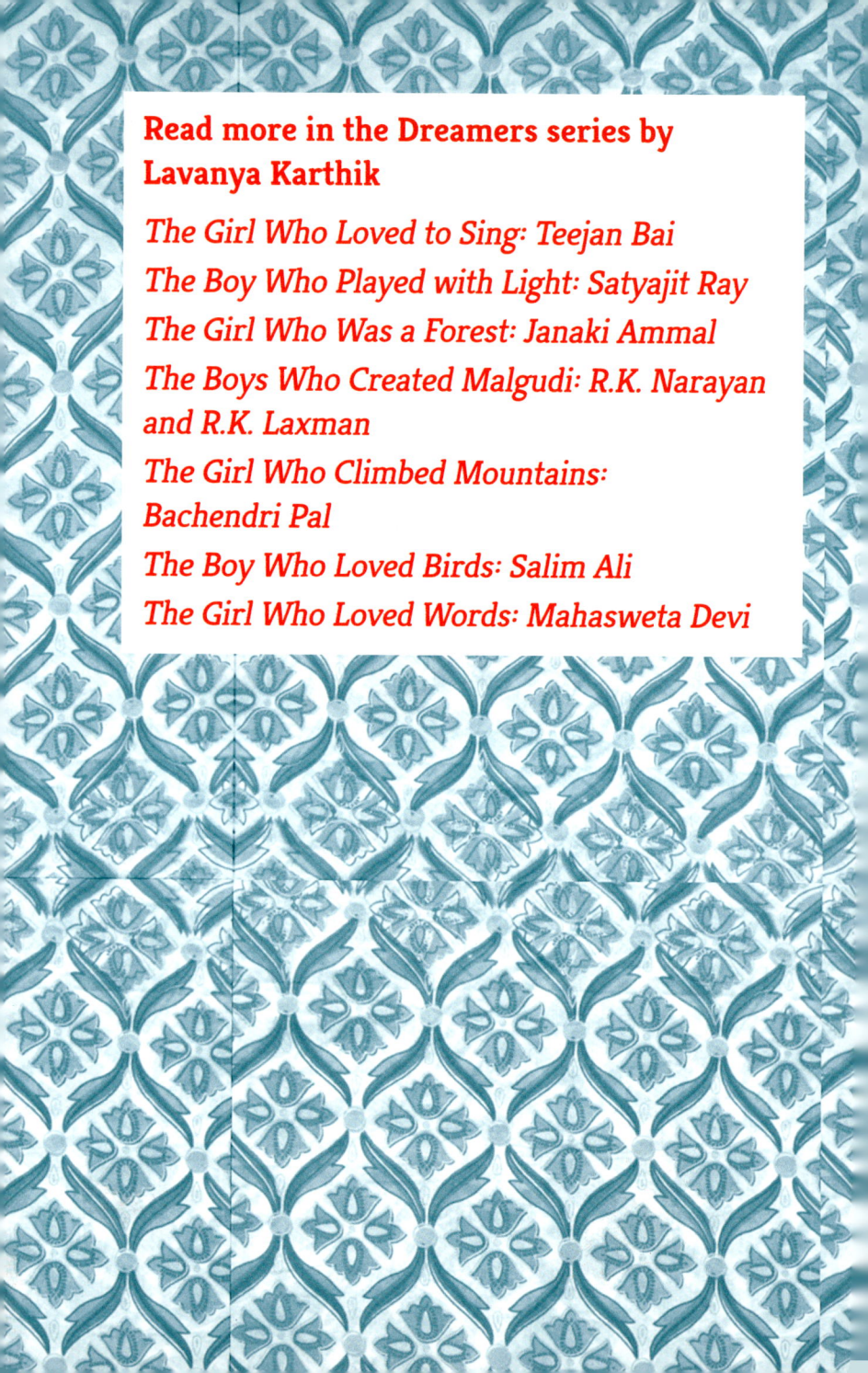

THE BOY WHO MADE MAGIC

P.C. SORCAR

Written and illustrated by

LAVANYA KARTHIK

An imprint of Penguin Random House

For you and the magic in your heart

DUCKBILL BOOKS

USA | Canada | UK | Ireland | Australia
New Zealand | India | South Africa | China | Singapore

Duckbill Books is part of the Penguin Random House group of companies
whose addresses can be found at global.penguinrandomhouse.com

Published by Penguin Random House India Pvt. Ltd
4th Floor, Capital Tower 1, MG Road,
Gurugram 122 002, Haryana, India

Penguin
Random House
India

First published in Duckbill Books by
Penguin Random House India 2022

Text and illustrations copyright © Lavanya Karthik 2022

ISBN 9780143458425

Typeset in Georgia by DiTech Publishing Services Pvt. Ltd
Printed at Paras Offset Pvt. Ltd., Kundli (Haryana)

www.penguin.co.in

Gili gili gili . . . choomantar!

Ladies and gentlemen, boys and girls . . . prepare to be amazed!

Turn the page to read a tale of magic and wonder! Meet the man who took Indian magic to foreign shores, and changed the world's image of Indian magicians—P.C. Sorcar.

But before he became Jadusamrat, the Emperor of Magic, he was a boy called Protul.

This is his story.

The circus was in town!

And with it, the Greatest Magician of Bengal . . .

GANAPATI CHAKRABORTY!

Everyone in Calcutta came to see him . . . and he did not disappoint.

Coins vanished!

Cards flipped and flew!

Everything seemed to dance to his tune!

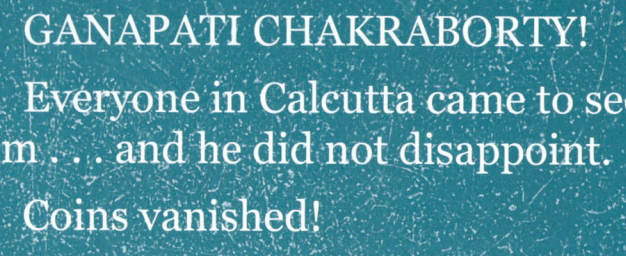

The crowds roared in approval—
well, almost everyone. The British
thought little of Indian magic, and
the people who performed it.

Later, a young man came to see Ganapati at his home in Calcutta.

'I want to be a magician like you!' he said. 'Please be my teacher.'

'Show me what you know,' Ganapati said.

The boy drew out a deck of cards.

Ganapati watched as they flipped, flew and

vanished between his nimble fingers.

'Hmmm,' he said, when the boy was done. 'Not bad. Now tell me, where does magic begin?'

'In my fingers!' the boy grinned.

'Wrong!' said Ganapati. 'Tell me, what else you can do?'

'I'm good at maths,' the boy replied. 'Best in my school! Think of a number, sir!'

3.1415676

67435

The boy was good! He made all the numbers Ganapati gave him dance to his tune.

'Very good!' Ganapati was impressed. 'But tell me, where does magic begin?'

336789

3435 856

The boy drew a coin from Ganapati's ear.

'In the audience's eyes!' he said and opened his palm. The coin had vanished!

'Good trick, wrong answer!' said Ganapati. 'You get one last chance!'

Sweat gleamed on the boy's forehead. His hands shook. He brought out a handkerchief and an old metal key.

Gili gili gili! Choomantar!

With a flourish, the boy lifted the handkerchief . . .

Clunk!

The key fell to the floor.

Ganapati sighed. So many young boys came to him, asking to learn magic. So many boys, wanting to be the next Great Magician.

'Try again!'

Once more, the boy lifted the handkerchief. And once more . . .

Gili gili . . .

CLUNK!

Ganapati sighed again. India was the birthplace of magic. But Indian magicians struggled to survive under British rule. Perhaps the boy would be better off learning a different trade.

'In the heart,' the boy said, clutching the key to his chest.

'Hmm?'

'In the heart,' the boy said again. 'That's where magic begins.'

'What do you mean?'

'Magic . . . it needs love, sir. And faith. If I believe in it—truly, with all my heart—the rest of the world will believe it too. Magic must begin—right here.' He patted his heart.

Ganapati looked at the boy. He took in his neat but old clothing and well-worn shoes, and noted the light in his eyes.

'Try again,' he said.

Once more, the boy set the key down, laid the handkerchief over it, moved his hands with a grand flourish, and . . .

CLUNK!

Silence filled the room. Slowly, the boy collected his things and walked to the door.

'WAIT!'

'You are right,' Ganapati said. 'Magic needs love, and it needs faith.

'It also needs practice. And a good teacher. We will begin on Monday.'

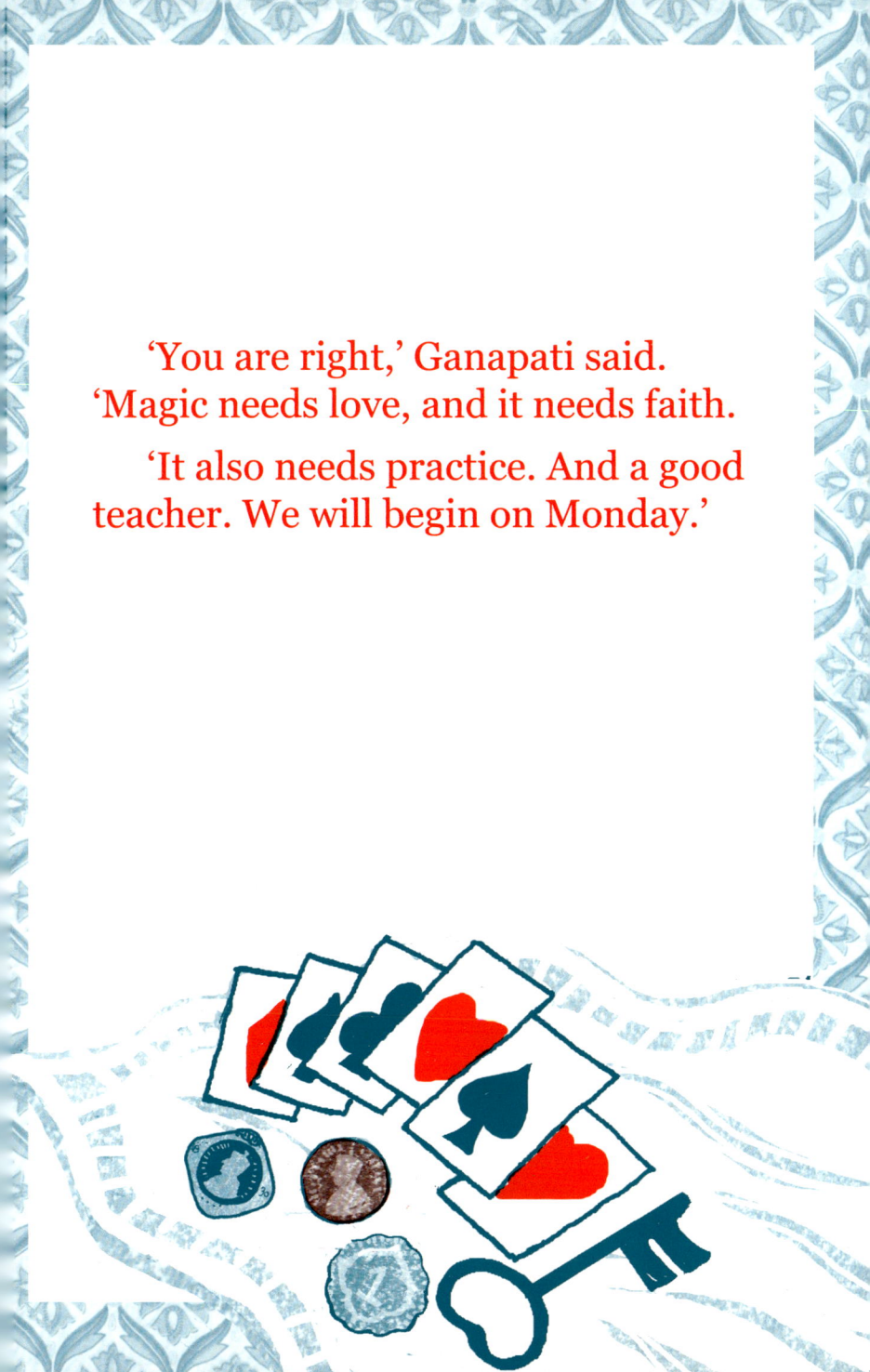

'You didn't tell me your name,' Ganpati said as the boy turned to leave.

'Protul, sir,' the boy replied. 'Protul Chandra Sarkar.'

'I don't hear the magic,' Ganapati said. He patted his heart.

For a moment, Protul looked confused. Then he nodded.

'Jadusamrat!' he grinned.
'Jadusamrat Sorcar!'

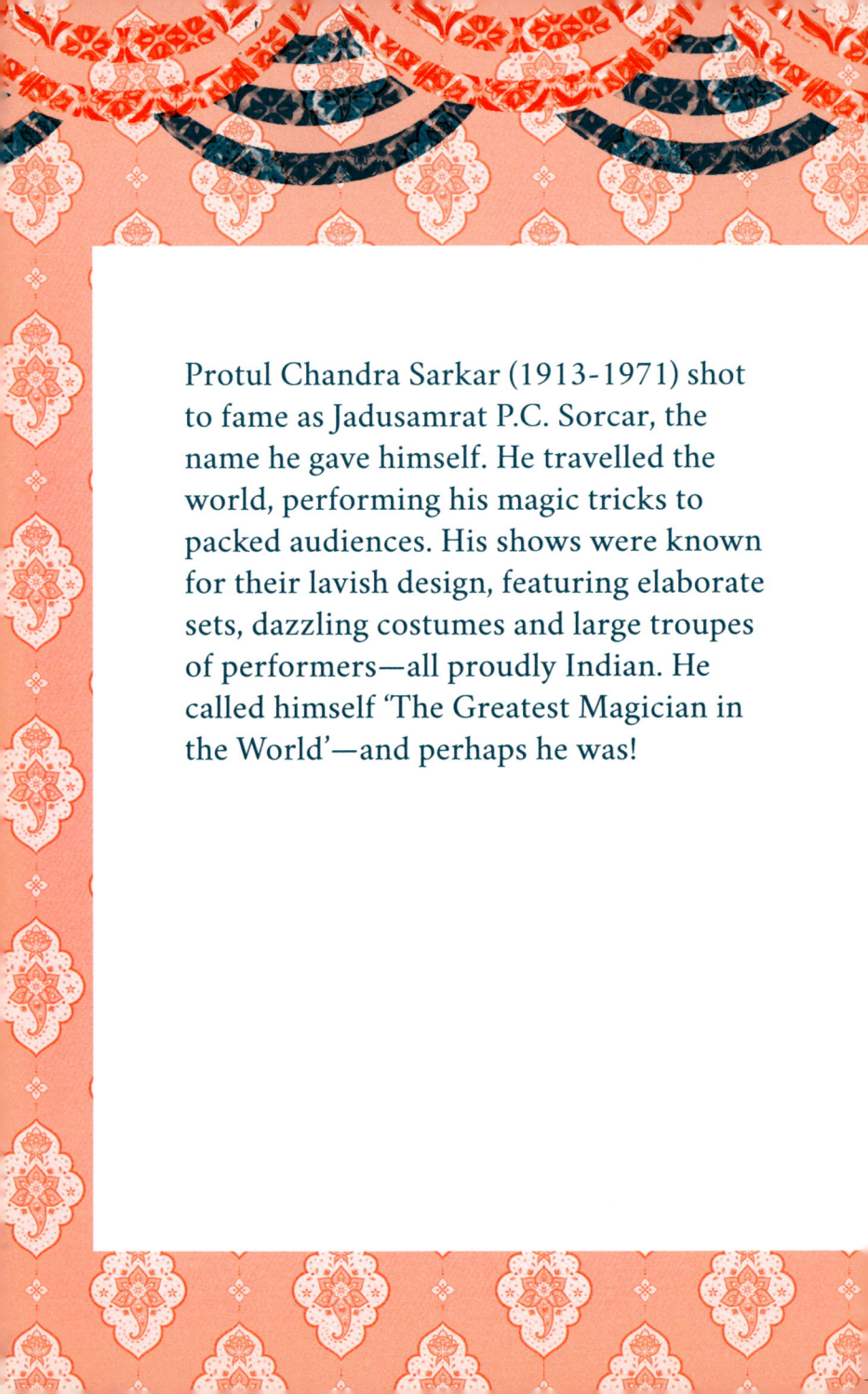

Protul Chandra Sarkar (1913-1971) shot to fame as Jadusamrat P.C. Sorcar, the name he gave himself. He travelled the world, performing his magic tricks to packed audiences. His shows were known for their lavish design, featuring elaborate sets, dazzling costumes and large troupes of performers—all proudly Indian. He called himself 'The Greatest Magician in the World'—and perhaps he was!

He was awarded a Padma Shri in 1964, and numerous honours, like The Sphinx and the Royal Medallion from institutions of magic around the world. A major street in Kolkata is named after him.

Babu Bibi paintings are a humorous genre that evolved from the Kalighat school of painting in Bengal, where Sorcar and Chakraborty lived. They are the inspiration for the illustrations in this book.

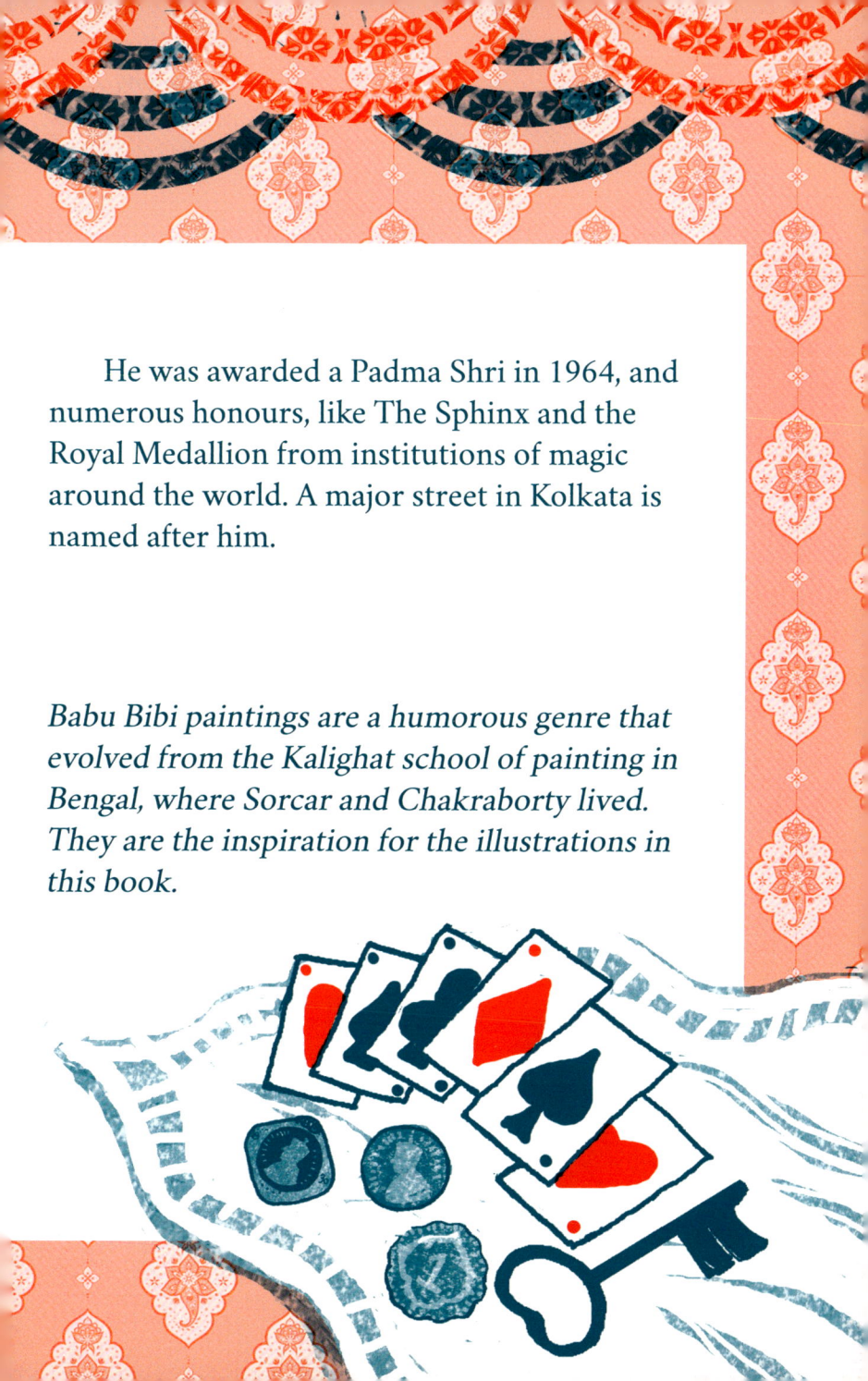

Lavanya Karthik is an author and illustrator by day, a cookie monster by teatime, and fast asleep by nine at night. She lives in Mumbai where she eats a lot of chocolate and takes a lot of naps.